FIREWEED

FIREWEED

Poems

William N. Gates

SUNSTONE PRESS
Santa Fe

Sunstone books may be purchased for educational, business, or sales promotional use.
For information please write: Special Markets Department, Sunstone Press,
P.O. Box 2321, Santa Fe, New Mexico 87504-2321.

Book and cover design › R. Ahl
Printed on acid-free paper

Library of Congress Cataloging-in-Publication Data
Names: Gates, William N., 1930- author.
Title: Fireweed : poems / by W.N. Gates.
Description: Santa Fe : Sunstone Press, [2019]
Identifiers: LCCN 2019006385 | ISBN 9781632932600 (paperback : alk. paper)
Classification: LCC PS3607.A7888 A6 2019 | DDC 811/.6--dc23
LC record available at https://lccn.loc.gov/2019006385

WWW.SUNSTONEPRESS.COM
SUNSTONE PRESS / POST OFFICE BOX 2321 / SANTA FE, NM 87504-2321 /USA
(505) 988-4418 / ORDERS ONLY (800) 243-5644 / FAX (505) 988-1025

For Helen

CONTENTS

Part III – Citations

Fireweed

Part I – Layers

AGES AND AGES

Overlapping scales
Of fish, feathers, shingles,
Waves in sequence rolling,
Generations fanning out—

1940
Little boys finger-whip
Each others' rumps and jab
Their knuckles into arms,
Snap their towels at buttocks,
Jeer at one another
"Can't you take a joke?"
Somehow they become fathers.

1964
Amy slaps her hand
On table and declares,
(bang) "BOP-ee!" "BOP-ee!"
As soon as she can walk
She leaves the house in diapers,
And on her own she goes
Exploring the terrain.

1988
Knees pumping, Mark
Scrambles across the floor,
Stops at grownup feet,
Looks up and sits, one leg
Bent, the other straight.
When hands raise him up
He bounces wildly, roaring.

1995
When Emma eats, she tenses,
Quivers, whacks the high-chair.
Gnaws on toughest toys
To test her tiny teeth.

She chortles and she growls,
Sheds big tears and gives
Lusty wails of sadness.

2010

At 80 all is past,
Swamped in memory.
The present is a moment
Ever burning, blackening,
Flimsy news. The future's
Fixed, with visible limits,
Not much mystery there.
But a child is swamped
In present, avoiding bullies,
Stuck in books of problems,
What to do today.
The past is in the making,
The future is opaque except as it is written
In the faces of our grandmas.

Allendale Street

Still daylight when I went
To see the doctor;
Forty minutes later,
Outside it was dark,
Not even sundown but
A blink back to old Time.
Driving along, the uncommon
Twilight of Santa Fe
Put me in a strange
But familiar neighborhood
Where I'd lived one time
In '63 with Ann
And our three little ones,
6 and 3 and 3 months.
The time flick tricks me,
Dusk ordains the light
Of 6 o'clock, November 3,
I'm driving back to our rental
On a street called Allendale,
Just around the corner.
Next spring I'm pledged to start
An adobe house for us
Which I don't have a clue
About, let alone to do.

Ann labors in the kitchen,
Amy shrieks in her high-chair,
Sarah reads "Goodnight Moon"
To Michael, I take to the piano
To a song called "Lonesome Road."
And all that's going to happen
Pours back in,
I know the future:
Kennedy will be killed;
I will build the house;
The children will grow up;
Ann and I will part;

And war will follow war.
The bolt of recall will shock,
Transform the life to come.

FATHER
1900–1988

Stumps endure more stubborn than stone.
The root wood makes a monument
Pointing upward long after tree
Has stretched its cracked parental length
Across whatever ground, attended
By its green and prickly offspring.

We came to visit in the ward,
Found him flat and very still,
His upward jut of nose a landmark.
"He's not even breathing," I said.
"He's dead," Bob said. And left to go
And bring the others. I stayed with him,
Touched him gingerly and poked.
His brow was cool, not cold, his mouth
Ajar, his teeth in place. I found
And held his hand, swollen, limp,
Unlike its knobby, rugged life.
The pulse had just withdrawn from him
And left a waxwork, as Bob said.
Which, converted into ashes
Would be sown in Buzzard's Bay,
Home of flounder, skate and scup
He'd taught us how to catch by hand-line.

He was thin and spare of build,
A gaunt Ohio Fred Astaire.
Coming home from work, he'd hug us
Hungrily with smacking kisses,
Hard and raspy evening cheeks.

Eccentric to his time and place
He craved a peaceful family life,
Governed by love and priggish regard

To budget, wrist-watch, thermostat.
He wore his underclothes to rags.
An antic spark in him burst out
In masquerades of Groucho, Gandhi,
Edith Sitwell. Of all the arts
He prized the Dance. Tweaked his trousers
At the knee. Creased his "Times"
As slim as he, so not to trespass
On his rapid transit neighbor.
At noon he steered away from colleagues,
Went to lunch alone and cheap.

"Good Night," he cried, to curse
A balky car or a wayward child.
Wordsworth was his thesis, law
His daily labor. Never in war,
He toured the battlefields of France
And wrote, "The glamour of war is gone."
Romantic novice when he wed,
Mismated from the painful start,
Within a year she loved another,
Yet he held her in the wedlock
Embedded like a knife in him,
Until their only child was eight.

Re-wed at 38, his bride,
Before so witty and alluring,
After grew so moody, touchy.
"I like to fight," she goaded him.
But with a modicum of rows,
With nervous delicacy she ruled.
No peace, his children gave him grief.
No escape from fractious life
Even in his "Golden Years."
And she, ever at war with herself,
As if to counter or erase
Her long-held grudges, would exclaim,
"Fifty years of that wonderful man!"
Dispersed in sea, rest in peace.

DEPARTURE

In light of lamps   platform
sleeper   going to board
wait till porter makes up berth
Father tells me what to tip
snowfalling light   train waits
comes snow descending   long
curves bending breeze
overnight sleeper   back to school
final hug   smell his cold wool
overcoat   climb aboard
peek out   still there watching
ski cap   earflaps down   hands
in pockets   still wartime
winter of 1945

Faraway Mourner

Beside the creek of Columbine
Not a crier but I cried.
Never saw my father cry
But suppose he must have done.
A tear, whatever he could muster
After the defeats of youth.

Here was far from ceremony
There on grass outside their house.
Clouds drooped and darkened on us
But refrained. We read his chosen
Words to family gathered there.
Elizabeth, Sarah, Bob and I.

Here was resonance of healing.
Recalled a time before when water
Healed me whole and strong enough
To wander in these mountains, find
Forgiving streams. Liquid music
Laid me open to my tears.

HOUSES
1770–1990

Trembling floorboards underfoot,
Cobble-bobble of crockery pitcher
In its basin, delicate
Tings of hangers tangling in
A wardrobe, restless window panes
For a desponding sky to show
Spidery cracks across the plaster:
"This is where you'll sleep," he says.
Outdoors he guides his cousin to
The fenced-in family burial ground
Concealed in weeds. "More are here
Than show," he says. He likes it so,
Exhausted house and secret dead.
Cost too much to fix it up
But they will go on living in it.
He seems to approve this fading-out
Of his ancestral line.

Houses
1830 – 1935 – 2010

The old house threshold, a step
Of stone leads down into
The Twentieth Century, across
A connecting hyphen where
The table of the telephone
Wobbles at a tiptoe and
A 'modern' grandma'd sit and chat
Cross-country to her sisters;
And a bookcase, twelve blue
Volumes of the Civil War
(Her father was a soldier in it),
And a cabinet with a mandolin
That resounds of former wooing;
Past the dining room and kitchen
Her mother added (1917);
On upstairs to more evolving
Bedrooms for her multiplying
Grandchildren, nephews,
Great nieces and collaterals.

Houses
1835 – 1900 – 1960

Once there was a cleric, classics
Scholar, abolitionist
Who built a simple clapboard house,
Who dug a tunnel for escaping
Slaves that led them to a river,
To Lake Erie and to Canada.
Then his grandson made a pile
In advertising; took the house
And made it bigger, made it grand,
Added portico with fluted
Columns and a pediment
(inside, triangular space for storage),
A sun porch and a servants' wing,
All painted white as wedding cake.
The bride and last old mistress died
In '54, the heirs bequeathed it
To the local women's club.
Coal-burning town and modern times
Begrimed it and surrounded it
With high-rise towers, parking lots
That stripped away its elms and lawn
And left it small, alone and fragile.

Houses
1840 – 1961 – 1995

Ocher bricks from natal earth
Constructed this enormous place
That five generations lived in.
Abundant lands were worked by slaves
The owner freed before the War.
(Twelve miles north a famous
Slaughter-field became a park
And glory story for the future).
Plenty of space attracted things,
China, tables, linens, pictures,
Years, which toted up three stories
Crammed the attic. As one would say
"Even if your house is huge,
In a hundred years you've got
Enough." No need to buy a thing.
The fourth and final heir arranged
The massed books by floor: first,
For classics, history; second, novels,
Mysteries, humor; third, children's.
Tacitus up to Trollope, Wodehouse
Up to "Through the Looking Glass."
The final heir died young, the widow
Couldn't cope and sold the place.
Years it waited until bought
By a hustling couple who would
Pour in money, refashion it
For honeymooners and conventioneers,
Add extra buildings to contrive
A Greek Revival Williamsburg.

Houses

1940 − 1970 − 2005

No doubt the neighbors snubbed
The staring white cube
So aloof and rudely
Modern. Yet its point
Was to break with the past,
To build a theater
Of less: plain elements
Admired for themselves −
White walls outside and in,
A window wall of glass,
A simple curving mantel,
Natural wood; a rounded
Wooden rail that zoomed
Upstairs along a steelwork
Banister; sliding doors,
Translucent glass, to veil
The dining space beyond.
The least obtrusive setting
For picture, object, people,
The actors in the play.
They would add the color −
Cool pink for entrance door,
A few choice paintings,
Off-white carpet, silver grays
For couch and chairs. Tall
Beige drapes unfurled at night
Across the naked glass.
Breaking with the past,
They wanted rest from color.
Much as they loved their place,
After thirty years
And children growing up
They sold and moved away.
New owners telescoped it.
And when last looked for

The house had disappeared.
Razed, erased as if
It never could have been.

Dream of Leavings

Wood
Dead   dear
Branches   brush   boards   bark
I stood them up
Embraced   leaned   lined
Wall   floor   my house no more
Roofless   wide to sky
For elements   to inspect
Castoffs   clothes   shoes
Little sandals   her old stuff
I tossed   piled
Maybe next people   would take
Beads green   blue
I picked them up
Pretty   take them
But she indifferent   busy
Playing   I said
I clung to every thing when I
Was discarded   single again
Now pile it up
Let it go

Our house is so precisely placed
Upon its land, its apertures
So aligned that we each March
Await a beam of setting sun
Which probes along the hall, searches
Through a door and finds within
The room beyond, upon a chest
Two enchanted Chinese courtiers
Carved in wood, ten inches tall,
And puts their perfect stately shadows
Sharp against the wall behind.
We know this searching will return
September next, inclined to winter,
We court the observance of the sun.

"Des pas sur la neige"
triste et lent

To make a mark in pristine snow
Untouched except by tracks of bird,
From this imagine creep of tree's
Long shadow toward the dark:
His music steps slow, mournful,
Steady, probing tone by half-tone,
Chords modulate those steps,
Color them in a kind of dirge.

Sometimes after snow has settled
Its silence over every thing,
Sometimes in this land all white
From mesa up to mountaintop,
I see the morning of the world
Before humanity, I almost
Can believe, before illusion melts,
Retreats, reveals what's underneath.

The headless ghosts not only fill
Our white deck chairs but overlap
And smother them, their round knees
Curve to lavish skirts that hide
Their feet. Conversation languid,
White on white, hovered over
By muffled polar paws that droop.
By and by come puffs of air
To nudge the wads of snow off them,
Release the paws to spring and nod;
Then wind disperses all in stinging
Mists that twist and writhe away.

Dream of England 1940

Somewhere in the Blitz
A crippled station still
Caught trains, crumble though
It would despite the props
Of plank that shored it up.
Under a splintered roof,
Wild for destinations,
People sought for word;
The clock was on the blink,
The voice of guidance silent,
The station caught but could not
Point them where or when.

Wild Garden

So tired trudging up that trail
I found what I didn't know I sought,
A small and stony spring-fed garden,
Dabs of dark blue monkshood, licks
Of scarlet paintbrush, hot yellow helenium,
Mosses, grasses all from one
Intimately rustling source.
There I let go of sticks and pack
And put myself down upon a flat
Sun-basking boulder. Eyes closed,
Head drooped. Mind tending to drift.
(Also faintly impinging, a little
Light airplane buzzed around the sky
In and out of hearing.)

Movies taught us to make the snarl
Of warplanes, the dive bomber's blare.
Mr. MacMahon taught current events.
When I was a boy I fastened on mouths,
Shape and line of lips, some curvy,
Charming, others more like scars
Set to grapple with the times,
Geronimo's mouth, Sitting Bull's.
"Mister Mac" had a thin crack
In a mordant face, big cheekbones
Over sunken, sucked-in cheeks,
High broad brow, glasses, hair
Combed back. Quiet of voice
But with a biting emphasis.
We knew our enemy silhouettes.
The mimeographed sheets he handed
Out were lists of target cities
Of Axis Europe, which we were
To memorize: "Gel-sen-keer-ken"
"Saar-brooken" "Bo-loan-ya"
"Chee-veeta-veck-ia" he said
Carefully, slowly. We must attend.

"C - D - F" - piano notes
Recall that wartime, me at twelve
And a cluster of people who were mine
As I was theirs; no garden but
A living room where figures form;
I sound a name and a shape, a face
Appear, more crowd in until
My grandmother's house fills up with them.
Some are bound for war and some
Bound to stay behind and wait.
"C - D - F
C# - D# - F - "
Synchronized with breath, tempo
Of a steep climb, fitted to
The upward steps, patient, slow
To attain the persuading of the tiny
Streams and colors of the flowers.

LAYERS

A crumbling rust-red road across uneven
    Ground tells the fall of a fir.
Poles of aspen drop, one on another,
    Haphazard grid to balk a hiker.
The annual grasses rising and fading,
    Wild oats that arch and aim
Their seed to earth, tall cow parsley
    Lifting husks of florets: snow
Will press them down. Below these the layers,
    Packed years of leaves, rose hips,
Wood lily, penstemon, yarrow and aster,
    Harebell, hellebore, monkshood and vetch,
Shooting-star, coneflower, skyrocket gilia,
    Each with its particular cut and hue,
    White and ultramarine, purple, violet
Yellow and scarlet—
    Praise them every one.

MARY MAGDALENE
BY DONATELLO, 1454

Her left bare foot clasps a rock,
Her right drawn back mid-step,
She seems to falter, hands raised
Tips of fingers not quite touching.
Her hair cloaks her like ragged bark
That clings to a hulk of forest tree.
Out of wood he carved the hollows
Of her cheeks, the caves of eyes,
Two stubs of teeth in her lower jaw.
Yes, "Magdalene" – a war survivor
Beyond the confines of her legend,
She implores.

A gospel song we sang when we
Were training for a distant war:
"Gonna lay down my sword and shield
Down by the riverside,
Down by the riverside,
Down by the riverside,
Ain't gonna study war no more."
It seems men learn in old age only,
Too old to study war any more.
Alone she comes toward us pleading.

SILENT GENERATION

I hear these mutterings:
"At ease, disease"
"You better believe it"
        "Never happen, GI"
We *will* get the shaft"
"You don't know, do you"
"It'll be your ass and mine"

My brain breeds green men,
They fade toward the shade
("Got it made in the shade"),
Their garb drab green when new,
But washed, rewashed and bleached
To a wan tinge of sage;
Green caps on faded men,
They sang their marching songs:

"I don't know but I believe
I'll be home by Christmas Eve"

"I don't know but I been told
North Korea is mighty cold"

"It's no use in goin' home
Jody's got your gal and gone"

"Am I right or wrong?"
"You're right"

LIFE mag would dub them
'The Silent Generation.'
No refusal, no flag
Burned, they just went.
One remembered later
"I came home on Friday,
Went back to work on Monday."

Dream of Faith

Not new and shiny, worn and stained
The wooden-handled kitchen knife
I carried as I left the wandering
Old folk and alone went looking
For some unknown thing, searching
Out of neighborhoods and on to
Larger downtown blocks where square
Led on to grander square, at last
A great white church of grimy stone.
And I went toward it, big old knife
In hand.
And woke with this in mind:

I don't know but I believe
I'll be home by Christmas Eve

Mass Levitation

An Eyewitness Account
By the Master of the Saint Lucy Legend
National Gallery

Somehow the delicacy contains and trains
Complexity, in an articulate confusion:
Footing a crescent moon, modest Mary
Ascends from Earth, surrounded, plucked, caressed
By an ordered swarm of angels, wings
Spread, lifting in pairs, their dense skirts
Whipped up in precise volutes and angled swirls
While musical angels celebrate her rise
On viol, harp, clarion, flute and tambour:
Ethereal jam, all for her, meek
And mild, all for mothering that child.

PART II – RIO MORA

Above

Theater of ethereal
Flowing west to east
Shreds of being in the making
Tatters groping for a form

Below

Water gorged with snowmelt
Overriding sound
Confined to the shape it carved
Rushing set in a constant form

AIM

Somewhere between improvisation and verse,
To merge the worked precision of the one
With the unworked fortunes of the other,
Somehow to meet the hard demands of both,
The rapids of awareness racing down
Their way around and over every stone,
The urge to pilot them toward a course
Of lines that when they reach a certain point
Turn back in measured pulse to bring along
The next and next in the switchbacks of a
poem:

Shock and ache of hands
I dip in ice-cold power
Paused in a pool backed up
Behind a wrecked fir;
The water circles, finds
Its dodge, spills out sideways.
Within the rapids' rumpus,
Islanded midstream,
Springing nonetheless,
Tall magenta primrose,
Greens of hellebore.
They dip their roots, they thrive.
So will I contrive.

EARLY MISERY

Life is streaming away
Through you and me, we're conduits
For its hidden rush,
Some swerves aside into
The curve of recall where present
Pushes past then comes
Around again for later
Review and second thoughts:
Walking along a certain
Street past certain houses –

The roofs are muffled, sidewalks
Crumpled paths, galoshes'
Buckles click as I track
The molded leaves of snow.
Out the upstairs window
My father is yelling "Go on,
Go on," but I'm dawdling,
Don't want to go to school.
He yells and waves me on,
My eyes and nose are running
And mittens can't console them.

FATHERING CHILD

Stuck in a grimy Ohio town,
Beguiled by 'Arizona Highways,'
I begot in me a parent
Who would take me out of where
I was and who I was, bespectacled
Boy with trapped and wired teeth.
He hummed a certain wordless song,
Hymn to the sacred far-off land,
He wrote a roster of tribes and chiefs.
And found a way by kindly friends,
A '41 Plymouth, the Shepherds
At the wheel, Pete and I in back,
To chug across three tedious states,
The Mississippi and the Platte
Until at last we came upon
A prickly pear and yucca spikes.
I smelled and stroked the gray-green sage
And Mrs. Shepherd sang, "Goodbye,
Old Paint, I'm a-leavin' Cheyenne."
Then first buttes appeared, the outposts,
And I began to yell and whoop.
Blessed ghosts of Mr. and Mrs.,
My thanks were in those happy shouts.

I was just eleven then,
Pilot child who put me West.
Now when I cross the Rio Grande
Through a gateway made of mesas,
The one to north rears up high,
My eyes climb its earthen ankles,
Up the knees and lap, up shoulders
To the rock of distant visage.
And I imagine some child playing
At adult feet, and peeking up
To a face that looks, listens, muses
Beyond defeat, remote, aloof.
Red Cloud, or could be Crazy Horse.

The Yardboy and the Starlet

Only five, was Jenny,
Child with azure eyes;
Dark hair cut short.
How could she take to him,
Fourteen, grubbing up weeds
In their enormous lawn
For a quarter an hour?
Nothing better to do
Than to come and fall
And sprawl all over him
As if he were her bear.
Her mother told her to quit.
He called it was okay,
Crouching over dandelions
While she poured herself
Upon his back and shoulders,
Tumbled off and climbed
Back on again; it seemed
She couldn't leave him be.
How answer lavish love?
(A word he never spoke
And one she didn't need).
"You made me love you,
I didn wanna do it,
I didn wanna do it"
The radio sang in wartime.

Before her nap she hung
Around him while he ate.
One time he pinched her hard
And made her cry, and he
Was wretched, he took her
In his arms and hugged her.

They never would meet again.
Nor would he meet her like
Till he was fifty, old
Enough for all-out love.

The Why-Not Step

Her name was Connie Kuhl
And she was very cool,
My classmate's date, already
Beyond and free of school,
At RISD, likely twenty,
Slim and aquiline,
Beaucoup de savoir faire;
They played "Tuxedo Junction,"
She taught me a sidestep,
Le pas de pourquoi pas,
She held me close, cheek
To cheek, her right foot
Crossed her left foot,
Her left behind her right
In supple sequence sideways,
Slinky, sexy, so
Advanced, she glided me
Through the box steppers,
Slow swayers, hands clasped
Doing the Frankenstein,
Through them all we *pourquoi*
Pas'd, and saw her boyfriend
In the stag line grinning,
Pink with jealousy.

SONATINE, RAVEL, 1948

"Sonatine" streams in me,
Boscastle, Cornwall, sun and sea.
I dropped my bike and dared the edge
Of a deep-down cove. Far below
Green waves were pushing in, and gulls
Were wheeling, screaming. Farther out,
A massive island rock alone.
I was eighteen and on my own.

Cycling down the Cornwall coast
My friend and I found out we couldn't
Stand each other. He quit and left
And I was glad to be alone,
Eager for Tintagel Castle
Down the way, Jamaica Inn
Somewhere out on cloudy moors.

But breakdown would not be forgotten,
No thought of one without the other.
"Sonatine" will sound them both.

Matisse Est Mort
(Headline Seen in Passing)

Jubilant, no more army,
Sprung I was, alive in Paris,
Metro humming, *pissoirs* busy,
Glorious glass of Sainte Chapelle;
Lots of laughs, old friend and I,
From GI chow to the best in the world,
We made the rounds of Loire chateaux;
Looking to Rome, then voyage home,
Family Christmas, Iowa workshop,
Learn to create on the GI Bill,
And other common ups and downs:

A kind of crush, Gloria by name –
Sic transit Gloria who?
Jones, good-looking, tall, blonde,
Shingle-bobbed a la '54;
Aboard that ship we sailed for France,
Nights we danced on a floor of glass,
Lights were glowing underfoot;
And yet when feet came to streets
We met just once, a cold November
Night, she wore a long gray cloak;
We walked beside the Seine, spoke
Hardly a word. And at the door
Of her hotel no numbers asked,
No future offered. Bye, how nice
To see you again, bon voyage, etc.

Matisse no more
Matisse est mort
11-3-54

Taos Fiesta, 1956

All that night we partied, then
I drove us out beyond the town
And parked us at an overlook.
Dawn was swelling over skyline,
Posing peaks against the light.

The jagged crack of Rio Grande
And surrounding miles of sagebrush
Were emerging from the dark.
A planet hung above the east,
Larger, more glistening than a star.

She was nineteen, blonde and hazel-
Eyed, a novice actress, "Becky"
For the stage. Her summer theater
Had closed and she would leave today
For home, Chicago and a boyfriend.

She lay across me close and tight
Behind the wheel. I was drunk
On her, her mouth, her arms, her un-
American, deliciously
Unkempt armpits. She named me

Her "*bête d'amour*," I told her that
I loved her. "Don't say that to me,"
She muttered. But I meant it all,
Avid for her and the dawn.
I almost cried to see her off.

The need to mollify the hurt
Was so acute that when she phoned
And said, "I want to marry you,"
It was too late, I had already
Found the woman I would marry.

"That was fast," said bitter Becky.

But just as soon she did the same.
Things collapsed so quickly then,
To right themselves as speedily
In the frantic, fatal search for solace.

Love's Highflier

My friend was always ready for love,
As one collapsed another raised him.
And now he launched himself again.
Late at night we heard his hushed
Telephoning in the dark.
From my protective cage of unhappy
Marriage I looked on amazed.
What was his secret, what was 'love'?
But there's no cutoff point for love
As even I was soon to find.
She could, she can, she will come along
And seize you, lift you high above
Her head, and bring you slowly down
Gazing into you all the while.

LOOKING BACK
ON COMING BACK

How could he have known, since
He didn't want to know but hoped
For things to normalize and settle.
His journal told him nothing new
So then a shock to look away,
Flash another scene, one year
Later—same set, rental decor
Of pallid drapes, neutral shag
Wall-to-wall—
And there he was, by himself,
Into an adventure, Nina,
Decades younger and divorced,
An eager stranger and a leap
Away from his wife of decades
(Who's into an affair), in trial
Separation (or a gap
Now widening rapidly, marriage
Already torn [he wouldn't see]
To bits, abandoned [surely they'd
Pull back together]) but stuck
In their old complex (they have split),
And he's come back to this odd
But familiar town; now he's renting,
Others live in the home he built,
Some accept him, some retreat,
One assures him, "Some of us
Are on your side" (and what's more
The young and supple divorcee
Awaits, primed and ready for action).
Things are moving fast, leaving
Him behind, he must catch up,
Take part (but he's fifty and
A stranger in his own life).

The Approach

The years have blitzed their way through here,
Snapped and felled trees athwart
The trail that was, the sweet remote
I'm searching for. Was it here
Or farther up the two of us
Began our kiss. No telling now,
Time has chomped away the path.
What I will keep is our approach,
The query of eyes, advance of touch,
The slow seeking push of lips.

BEGINNING

Then we embraced, and we
Imploded, fused, made
Mysterious exchange:
You gave yourself to me
But also gave to me
Myself as well as a life
I'd never mused could be;
And I gave you the same,
Miraculous swap,
Of potence long unknown
To us and now released.

Sierra

Means "saw" as with
The peaks of your
Precise incisors,
Childhood saw-points
Unworn, unground,
Unique and precious
Serrated charms
Each child may have
But cannot keep,
You have kept
Despite the dentist's
Urge to smooth
Them out. Never:
Immortal now
We must preserve
From orthodontic
Betterment.

Rio Mora

Illusion of inexhaustible pleasure,
The constant wave that crests, curls,
Conquers the up-push of smothered rock,
Wave ever bucking, breaking, staying,
Never spent.

We cat foot out along a log
That leads to a stony midstream shoal
And take each other in embrace
All the more pressing, not being young,
All intent.

Time might roll over us, leave us
There, a piece of passing driftwood.
But the power of love is in us,
Through the clamor of the water
I hear your voice defying time
In fierce consent.

Keep In Mind

In a Time of Discord

Do you recall that mountain flank
All feathered with the changing aspen,
Cool to scorching under cloudy
Dark and desultory rain?
We crossed the Rio Santa Barbara
With sticks to hop slick rock
To rock to reach the further
Range of trail which led us up
Around a turn and then revealed
The unexpected lights of leaves
Overlapping, rising into mist.

Season
Solace

Discontent
Dissolved
Devolved
Speck
Sparks
Circling
Shady
Submarining
Shapes shimmy
Counter current
Aim upstream
Await
Foozling
Flies

Worries
Furies news
Defused
Eyes noses
Feel Fall
Seeds stick
Stamens stalks
Catch us
Patches yellow
Farewell
Smell
Descent
Scent

November Aspen

Eyes analyze
Slim shorn limbers
Many ways aisles
Perspectives intersect
Sight slight straggle
Down variable
Agreeable verticals
Permitting eyes to lock
On slimmest sunlit
Sliver far
Eyes seize
But sidewise blink
Budge lose
Lost

Amid muddled memory
Rift of music
Ear clears
Chords adored moored
Somewhere past
Something wherefrom
What after fades
Racket static
Closing over
Gone

Minutes Toward Night

White
flight-lines
write
acute
Xs
dissect
sky
vexed
eyes
burn
turn
snow
shows
tree-lines
far-flowing
undulate
relate
minúte
motion
mute
motive:
night

New Mexico in April

For seven starved months
The roadside trees reach
Haggard up to heaven,
They've really dried and died
Clawing at the clouds.

Despite the wind and dust
Sudden tiny leafies
Pop out along their branches,
Tease their dying drama,
Twit them to revive.

FAIRY SLIPPERS

The dream was in the confluence
Of elements and would continue
When we found ourselves again
In summer solstice light and shade,
In perpendicular woods, whose floor
Newly sprung, yellow green
Sloped steep across the trail,
Which after leading on a while
Revealed to us the little scarlet
Columbines with spurred bonnets
Nodding, and then one by one
The tiny purple fairy slippers
That lured us down upon our knees
To look and marvel at them close.

You recall it was a certain trail
That cut across a mountain's angle,
Descending gently through a grove
Where aspen sensed a breeze that we
Could not, but cooled us nonetheless.
Have we gone back that time of year
And to that place? No, not ever.

Fireweed

Salsify is ready
In its round gray shock,
And now arising from crammed confinement
Inside each red-purple tendril of split
Pod, emerge the massed fireweed seedlets,
Dark but with voluminous gossamer gowns
So ethereal that merest whims of air
Will lift them out on dainty excursions,
Random, vague: extravagant outpour
To give one mote of hope one chance
In all the miles of burned-up earth.

October Pilgrims

Despite the coming dark of clouds
We pushed on up the rudimentary
Forest road, a crowd all sorts,
Old as eighty, young as three.
Their parents let them race ahead,
One mother said, "It always happens,
They run and then it's 'Carry me'"
As she hefted up her boy.
A common yearning drove us: rare
To feel so warm and kindly mid
These many strangers, make them 'us'
And celebrate, as rain began,
The sudden brilliant slopes ahead.

As the Crow Flies

High up, mid-afternoon,
Trees still, air
Calm. Then a rush,
A horde of crows roars
Past, wings whipping
Wh – wh – wh – wh –
They scatter, circle, query,
Then gang together again
And fly away to the west.

I know where they're heading
And I will follow them
Across the roving sage,
Down to the dark brink
And rift of Rio Grande,
To glide out over the gorge
Where laps of shadow spread
A premonition of night.

Far below, the Rio
Feeds a ponderosa.
I nose its sun-warmed bark
To catch its vanilla scent,
I look up through its boughs
To see the rows and tiers
Of birds in glossy black.
I hear how they confer
In curious coos and squeaks,
Whistles and sounds like
A gritting of the beaks.

Sun sets early here,
And dawn arrives late,
Why not stay the night
Near water and maybe food,
With a *rio* of stars above
And room for all in the cloak

And long susurrus needles
Of this commodious tree.

And so our dreaming eyes
Can range the sixty miles
To a solitary butte,
And in the same gaze
Can follow the crows around
And around below the sun
And down to the riverine dark.

Part III – Citations

Tedium of Time

It just goes pounding on and on
Steady as car after car after car
(Except it's always growing louder),
While memory flits here and there
Imprisoned in the noise, in its shell
That tries to keep the outside out,
The inside in; caught but free
To skim and dodge decades, dive
Backwards, sideways, always erratic,
Lured by a name or a silly tune
(While the boom box beat closes in).

Brief

Routed out by daylight saving,
Dreams popped and atomized,
You push along a road still dark,
Pursuing work, appointment, errand
Past a life so used it's barely
Noticed—
          and even if examined
Gone as if it never happened.

BANDELIER
A CANYON STREAM

Leisurely, wily
It chafes and smoothes
Its way down deep
In volcanic crust,
This slim stream
Has raised parapets,
Turrets topped
By beaked gargoyles,
Has disclosed
Stained vertical
Tapestry stripes,
Ocher, carmine,
Caput mortuum,
Palisades now in
Turn being
Dismantled drop
By drop, rain,
Ice, wind-worn
Walls rise up
To be cracked,
Ground down.

BANDELIER, TOP LAYER

Perusing this tuffaceous rind
Of old and broken volcanic land,
Eyes approach a garden motley,
Huddled lichen gray-green-blue,
Burnt orange and chartreuse.
Close-up eyes scan the tuff
And catch a glint, an embedded eye
Of the great sun in pocked rock,
Which gleams again in black shards,
Obsidian for arrow points.

Shell of spruce so thin resounds
Marimba tones tapped at random,
Shape of spire or coyote snout
Lifted to yowl, hollowed, light,
Found among blooming gentians,
Spilled boulders.
At twelve thousand,
August 2002.

Intact relic of grain gray writhing
Like sea around rocks, so bound
Together, mating fiber to fiber,
Locked annals of parallel gnarling.
Found near worn-out gold workings.
Timberline, July 1989.

Two long splinters of fallen aspen
Balanced upright, crossed like teepee
Poles, slender three-foot wands,
Fleeting gray and faint clouds
Figured along their slim smooth skins.
Found above forks of Holy Ghost.
Nine thousand, October '99.

GOODS FROM THE WOODS

Smart start needs slivers brittles
Dry weeds snappish twigs
Spark sprigs mix thicker sticks
Words matchless scratch moods
Lug log pitch swatch
Sweat sap beads smear smell
Sear eyes cry smoke
Plunk poke big hunk hunker
Huddle close cluster gloods
Feed good words wood woo
Goods from woods

Monuments

Uptorn root
Rears up in dare,
Its dead mainmast
Disintegrates
To dirt, link
By link, chunk
To crumb. But root
Remains, gnawed
Sharp by weather
To elemental
Tawny resin,
Hard as horn,
Which ageless propped
A ponderosa
Against the push
Of western wind.
No less lasting
Than Pedernal,
El Cabezon
Or spired Shiprock,
That challenge us
To remember them.

CITATION

Deep below the windy bending aspen,
Fathoms down to bottom deadfall ground,
Lies a kind of Chinese wall, a trunk
Sprawled long and dark across the trail.
All its ages are crumbling to burnt umber
And to food for plants that flourish on it,
Mushrooms, mosses, trees from sprout to sapling
Taking hold in its enormous mulch.
Praise this surrender, this prolific hulk,
No tomb, no dirge, an unceremonious gift
Flung to all who'd eat its body and grow,
So grand, so rotten and so nourishing.

EACH PRECARIOUS

We each a tower of memory massed
As a tree trunk in the wilderness,
Riddled, reamed by the ants of recall
Pursuing blanked-out names and faces;
Each an ample whatnot, shelves
Packed with pictures, pills and bills,
Blouses, blackened baby cups,
Scissors, screws, shoes all sizes.
Heads taller than life we sway
And totter trembling, clinking along
Trying not to spill one hour,
One minute of our crazy loads:
The way we really look, not
Smiling shadows, precarious towers.

Sleepless in Baltimore

Spring and night are mingling
With aftermath of rain,
Our wide-arching window opens
To lean and breathe the wet.
What smell? Magnolia maybe,
Apple perhaps. The birds
Are sound asleep, but clamorous
Leaves are shedding drops,
A car hisses and splashes
Along the street below,
A train cries long
Jubilant wails through town.
Three o'clock and four –
Wide awake and music's
Chugging into mind –
Pinetop Smith, Freddy Slack,
Meade Lux Lewis,
Honky Tonk Train Blues:
A fanfare tremolo then
That rickety rackety bass
That runs a locomotive
With flourishes and off-beats,
Triplets in the treble.
Now it's slowing – pause –

Psssssh – station stop,
A riverine railroad town
Along the Susquehanna,
Other blues are sounding
From an all-night bar.
The tremolo cajoles
And Honky Tonk is moving,
It's swaying, unrelenting
Beats precise as pistons.
No piano here, but darkly,
Blindly my fingers reach
For notes. So long, night.

October Sumac

Rising and glowing in
An interstate interstice
Trapped between ramps
A crimson-feathered sumac,
And we trapped in traffic
Can only catch a glimpse,
No stopping no slowing, locked
Rushing past October.

Autumn City

Trek, track, tread, wade
The crimson trash of oak, and trace
Our whereabouts Novembers past.
The tulip poplars paste their yellow
Cutouts in a giant scrapbook;
Big as sheets of paper, bronze
Tinged with green, the sycamores
Are landing. Maple's lights come on,
Almost hot to step across.
They're drying after rain, our nostrils
Flare to catch their reminiscence.
They spread a Persian beyond price,
And rags and rot beyond woe.
Now the blowers are bellowing near.

Briefly air was in a whirl,
A getaway party in the sky.
Then they fell, they swayed their way
Past our windows, twirling tulip,
Rocking beech, each in the dance
It was born to do, landing last
Far from their beginnings, this shape
By that shape, drab side up,
Color side up, ocher, carmine.

Rest on the Flight to Egypt
—Veronese, National Gallery

Through doors of room beyond room
The color draws you from a distance,
Scarlet like an ibis glowing
Among drab pelicans: the garb
Of an angel attending the refugees.
Up in a palm, an orange angel
Dangles like a monkey picking
And dropping dates to those below.
The donkey is smiling. To the left,
In effulgent white, some swaddling
Hung to dry. You feel the ease
And cheer of a party, an Italian
Picnic that might be paused in flight.

Museum of Natural History
Drawing Lesson

Eyes align the vertebral links,
The crawling filaments of snake.
Poise the bulk of bear and rhino,
The rock-like pelvic girdle, scapula,
Skull. Trace the stilt, the bat
Tenuous as thread, how they spell
Skeletal airs, like wind playing
In bony twigs, harmonic hollows.

The task, to draw our old zoo friends
As specimens now stripped and scoured,
Rigged up in walk, flight, swim.
High on a wall, the seagoing dugong
Hung paddling, now a model
Of ancient age, with sunken cheeks,
Feeble flippers, prominent snout.
None is spared, all are there,
Our pencils stroke a way to adore.

CARDINALS IN THE RAIN

They're tuning up in winter melt,
"Wheet, wheet, tew-tew-tew-tew,"
Time to break their winter silence,
Time to mate: almost March,
Car splashing by in slush,
Raindrops' dim marimba on
The fire escape. In dawn murk
Our room is dark but light enough
To lift the puff that covers us,
Give it a shake to plump it up
And give me the view and array of you
In this persuasive semi dark.

ALMOST APRIL

Traced in snow, boughs of spruce
Droop and poise like talons,
Tentative. Cold and redolent
The late blizzard drips away,
Reviving wet black earth,
Pinks of weeping cherry,
Scatter of white dogwood
Among dark and naked trees.
At sunset we will see
Again the long-shadowed people
Walking in the park,
The tall-shadowed children running.

Spring Goodbye

Amid that everyday workaday town
Of sirens, leaf-blowers, garbage trucks,
The spring came on cold winds, silent
Fireworks of forsythia, magnolia,
Jonquils, dogwood, azalea in sequence
Bursting regardless against the dark
Still-wintry trees. But out our window
The tulip poplar launched its tiny
Leaves on stems that twirled and wagged
Like Italian hands in various
Moods. And as we packed the boxes
For our faraway move the mood
Was bent on leaving, also knowing
That we would lose the precious spring.

Faraway Friends

Life would seem a long span
But it's quickly gone. We meet again
Then rocket away back to other
Distant lives that gobble us up.
Maybe meet again twenty—
Thirty years later and now
We're 60 or 70, even
Our children are 30 or 40—
"I haven't seen you for years! How long
Has it been? We must not let
So much time go by. Bye-bye."

Home Country Song

Freed from eastward flatness, states
And cities masked in haze,
We embrace our mountain range,
A fleet of brilliant sails
In rocking journey north to south;
Such clarity of air
To breathe the mountains while our eyes
Possess the sight from patient
Rio nibbling at their feet,
On up the foothills, forest,
Crowns of snow. This our country's
Land in motion stilled,
Unresting quiet earth, our solace,
Our New Mexico.

DREAM OF LOSING

I dreamed our theater seats
Sat behind each other.
You wandered off, I saw
There was plenty of time
To go back and get
Some thing I had to have.
Outside the streets were dim
And dark, I took one leading
Uphill, with no sidewalk
So I must hug the wall.
The wrong way it seemed
And then around the corner
Came a streetcar brightly
Lit, an incandescent
Empty trolley, and
It missed me clinging to
The wall.

I never got
Whatever it was I needed;
(and you dreamed you lost me)
(while I was losing myself).

PIECES OF HOURS

To catch this sight before the dawn
We sneaked outdoors at 5 a.m.
(Quiet, don't set off the dogs)
To see the city of the stars.
Alive they wavered, brightened, dimmed,
And once in a while a dart of death.
Ursa Major had wheeled around
To north, Orion center stage.

A drink of water at 5 to noon,
A need to dunk my lips and nose
In a green glass rattling with ice.
I hardly dared to lift my eyes
To the wide adobe wall so burning
In the sun, to the fierce and cobalt
Blue above: one flash of them,
I dove back in the green to escape
From ocular delirium.

At 6 p.m. we saw a wave
Of cloud flown up in a crown of spray
That slowly drifted north to reveal
The hard, blue-white chip of moon.
The blown wave would hold its figure
Changing hue from gold to pink
While the chip grew harder, brighter
In this be-all end-all sunset
Of purple and orange, and way in a far
Corner a storm muttering, flickering.
We were there, we're here to tell you,
We heard the dogs and children shouting.

At 3 a.m. the slashes of moonlight
Wrecked the night in blobs and oblongs
That changed the house to a haunted day.
The dogs were out in depth, and now
The neighbor's little squealer joined,

Obnoxious pup amid the junk
Across the road, protecting a castoff
School bus, a carapace of car.

CROSSING A RIDGE

We crossed a ridge and put a mountain
Between us and the scarred, scourged
Ski valley in its racket of building,
And all we heard was the howl of a wolf
In the basin below the highest peak
And saw no person, no tree, just grassy
Massif of mountainous shoulders and arms,
And in its lap the wolf was crying,
And farther down where furthest timber
Reached, a dog was barking back.

Powerhouse of Clouds

Let us climb close to clouds,
Even in them taste
Their cold nuzzling mist,
And onward up to a clearing
To watch clouds build,
And bulge as taut and tense
As a nine months' belly's swell
Against the dark and gentian blue.
This radiant brooding rises
All the way to where
The high prevailing currents
Catch and sheer its crown,
Veer and streak it southward.

Another and another render
Tall showers to wander
This enormous earth,
To sway and dance upon
One prayerful patch and give it drink.
Some of us will revel,
Many cannot, and some will
Get a flood, their neighbors
Not a drop. This terrain's
Too big and harsh for millions
But may assent to the few
Who contrive to make it home.

TIRED OF FLYING

Up Big Tesuque Creek
Step by step we climb
Closer to the clouds,
Past the vertical tones
Of aspen winter-bare,
Ongoing tones of water
Filling ears and brain.

Tired of freeways, airways,
Skies wan as ash,
Crowds cold and hustling,
Thinkers sunk in gloom.
Why do we exist?
What's the point of it?
Is there no way out?

Up here where water reigns
Questions will dissolve
In circularities
Of froth.

Birthday

We climbed and you were strong,
Not tired or checked by pain,
Cheerful amid the trees
Alight with newborn leaves.
The wind swayed and raised
A chant, a vowel for
The day, your day of birth.

Thirty years before,
The summer we began,
We were walking toward
A concert in a crowd,
You said "I love you"
In a soft, downy voice
Searching in the dark.
You took the chance and won.
I still hear your voice
Braving all the future.